Satanic Witchcraft

Victor Barrett

"We, even the weakest among us, are better than the best of them." - Fiona Goode

Printed in the United States of America

First Printing, 2017 Seven Darks Press

SEVEN DARKS
PRESS

Contents

-1-

Dreams In the Witch House

It was during my preparation for initiation into a certain Coven back in 1983 that I had a dream which I would later understand as having great significance for me. It was night and I was with a group or men and women of various ethnicities and physical characteristics. The only thing we all had in common is that we were wearing black clothes and most had some kind of black head wear. We weightlessly flew in circles above some old suburban home and then five or six of us descended to a second story balcony and entered a dark bedroom through a set of glass double doors. One of the women stayed next to me and three others moved to a bed where someone was sleeping. The woman next to me turned to me an explained that the man sleeping in the bed was a rapist and we were there to remove his genitalia.

I was in awe of what I was experiencing. The three witches did the work on the sleep-paralyzed rapist and after that was completed we all silently floated out of the room and back into the moonlit night. I woke up form that dream knowing without a doubt and with every cell of my body what a Witch was, what Witches did and most importantly that I was and always had been one.

Every individual Witch has their own understanding and opinion concerning the definition of Witchcraft and magic. The entire concept of magic is both a highly personal set of interrelated ideas as well as a kind of force that has developed and gained momentum over thousands of years; a force that picks up the personal contributions of thousands of magical practitioners and changes as it moves through time.

Magic is the ability to use abstract, unknown forces in order to cause tangible change. I do not know precisely why magic works, and neither does anyone else. As we cleave into the future, I expect that we will make many significant discoveries regarding the nature and use of what we call magic. I also feel that when it comes to this elusive art form, some people simply have it and others do not. Yes, you are either born a Witch or you are born an average person with no Witchcraft potential. This does not mean that there are those among us who have been systematically browbeaten into burying their innate power and who have sought to flee from every vestige of their true nature.

I have been a natural warlock since childhood, and perhaps my inability to define magic in a completely precise way stems from the very nature of magic itself. For me, witchcraft is a barely describable feeling. It originates in the darkness and the energetic matrix of the elements and the earth and because the Witch is the Earth's ultimate ally, she has given us the distinct honor of being capable of channeling, magnifying and directing power in her and our own defense and for the fruition of our own objectives.

Witchcraft is synonymous with power, and because of this I believe a clear definition of such an abstract concept is indeed possible. The Witch has always been a figure viewed by the herd of humanity as someone who, whether alone or allied with a group of Witches is directly connected to unseen forces that imbue them with abilities unavailable to the average person.

Witches are generally feared, sometimes respected and usually hated outsiders moving in the shadows of the world and inconspicuously influencing people and events in accordance with their own ends or the objectives of the Coven to which they may belong.

This image captures the essence of what I understand to be the true classic Witch and Warlock; practitioners of Satanic Magic having the deepest connection to the earth, the elements, and their own carnal powers while solely concerning themselves with the pursuit of power and the ruin of modern humanity's selfish agenda to blaspheme and destroy all that is truly sacred.

Witches are the incarnated individual and collective expression of humanity's shadow self and as such we are the natural enemy of mankind. Most average people are generally confused as to what exactly a Witch is. The classic idea of the Witch lives within all of our thoughts, formed and molded by those images we primarily absorbed as small children. There has always been something about the archetypical image of the Witch that originates deep within the most ancient recesses of the human mind and experience.

The Satanic Witch and Warlock are anonymous wielders of power who delight in all things carnal and of the earth and who are directly connected to the elemental sources of power; power used to bring ruin to those who oppose them and to hasten the decline of ordinary humanity's ignorant and misguided ambitions in the beautiful world they systematically destroy. There have always been certain individuals born and walking among the ordinary herd of humanity; creatures that are born with and contain within themselves an unusual predisposition to attract an extraordinary, indefinable force. They have the mysterious ability to influence events and ordinary people in a peculiar and sometimes intangible way through the direct application of this unknown power. If the individual Witch becomes aware of this inborn capability, they can eventually groom their talents until they become a distinct and sophisticated endowment. The skilled Witch is truly akin to a living magnifying glass, concentrating the unseen powers of nature according to their own non-human ends.

My unwavering assertion as a Warlock concerning the rest of what is popularly referred to as the "herd" of humanity is that people are very simple and stupidity is not the exclusive trademark of the uneducated. The skilled Witch weaves even the most educated and renowned into their webs of intent. The primary difference for me is that I do not say this from a sentiment of emotionality or resentment. It is simply a fact that must be realistically acknowledged for our work to begin. We are the natural enemies of humanity because they have made us so.

Is this whole process reflective of our evolutionary path? Has our need for the expression and struggle of human excellence been surpassed by the pace of our advanced technology? In all reality this could very well be true, however there are bound to be a few major historical hiccups before we completely leave behind our need for true leaders and other vibrant, brilliant beings to guide the masses towards their unlikely survival.

There will most certainly come times when hordes of human beings, confronted with a new manifestation of nature tooth and claw, stand together with mouths gaping and not knowing what to do next. They will look to each other for direction and skill, but there will not be enough to go around because in our time we have selectively bred these traits out of ourselves and our children. All for the sake of the very strange ideas of this new world order. The human herd will be like lemmings, rushing over the cliffs of political correctness and dying the death of weak animals that have become distorted beyond nature. They have truly allowed the creation of a world where genuine talent is discouraged and is being hunted down to extinction.

Before we can effectively wield our inherent power we must first correctly understand that the "world" does not care about us as individuals and that any frustration we express in comparing ourselves to other human beings is an enormous drain of our most vital and precious energy. The first key to becoming a developed Witch is to completely and irrefutably remove one's self from the rest of the herd. I am trying to save my true sisters and brothers' years of anguish with this advice. Be rid of every degrading and common human affiliation that does not immediately lead to your well-being and happiness as the magical creature you are. You will NEVER fit in with them! Seek your power now and move among them quietly and with purpose. Hide yourself until your power is grown.

I know of individuals who profess highly developed mastery in the black arts who have floundered for years, teetering on the edge of acceptability and imagined notoriety while all along bringing home the same paycheck as those who got up early every day to put in the extra time that it requires to achieve excellence in any field of endeavor. It sometimes seems as if the less ambitious among us are actually rewarded for their inability to remain within what we have been indoctrinated to believe is the realm of the achiever. True creativity through the power of

Elemental Connectivity is the ultimate prerogative of the Satanic Witch and Warlock!

I have found that the dissatisfaction generally experienced by those drawn to the occult often stems from a problematic inner conflict between their own self-assessment as would-be practitioners and their actual effectiveness in the objective world. I am not writing this to insult fellow practitioners, however in order to help produce superior, self-realized Witches, unflinching self-honesty is absolutely necessary. One need not be a professional athlete, model, singer, etc. in order to achieve mastery in the black sciences but an inner, relentless striving for the betterment of one's conditions in this material world is critical. Without this inner passion, magic and sorcery are nothing more than an interest or curiosity.

I must say a word concerning religion. Religions have always been part of a strictly human agenda. I personally believe that a religious witch is one of the saddest things imaginable as this only attests to the religious witch's undeniable state of inner conflict. There are no gods; only power originating within and without and the true Witch is one who has become expert and plugging into this power. If you are someone who needs to believe that an omniscient anthropomorphic being is running the show then you a lacking one of the first fundamental characteristics of one who wields real power. A religious witch is a walking oxymoron.

This is not to discount the practices of evocation and invocation. While no true witch "worships" any deity, many among us understand the power that can be channeled from purposely focusing their intent on a potent exteriorized and symbolic representation of whatever kind of influence they choose to tap into. The images of Satan, Lilith, Hecate, Baphomet, etc. are focusers of attention, and as such they are the accumulators of power. These "beings" help us create the most ideal conditions for focusing our attention on aspects of ourselves and reality that ordinarily go un-apprehended and unused. The fastest way to tap into power for many is through repetitive ritual acts that have the unique capacity to focus attention in strange ways. These actions help us bypass the rational, herd mind and allow us direct access to power as it flows freely in ourselves and the universe.

Satanic Witchcraft is often concerned with handling people and it is employed in the world of ordinary affairs and on terms dictated by the governing physical and social rules of the time one currently exists in. One does not necessarily become a "master" of Outer Witchcraft; one is sustained and strengthened by its use and we can often gauge the witch's overall power by how well and to what extent they successfully employ this art. Lesser Magic is what I like to think of as social warfare in action.

It is utilized every day and at every moment, challenging us to assess what the next best decision is in any given situation and how we may stabilize and sustain the fruits of that action.

Yes, Lesser Magic primarily deals with the manipulation of people and events, but in order to be an expert social manipulator out in the world, we must first become master manipulators of the self; body and mind. Our inner world must reflect a precise order of our own construction so that our hearts are powered by the black flame itself and our minds are as vast pools of the blackest and stillest water. In this manner we will have nurtured the perfection of our own intent and we will sit in the eye of the storm, able to always command that which is without.

Satanic Witchcraft is a highly individualistic, dynamic and creative approach to existence and the challenges one encounters on it must be confronted. Nothing grows or changes without pressure being exerted. This pressure can be from without, or even from within one's self. Stagnation and orthodoxy are antithetical to the Left Hand Path. It is best for the Arte of Witchcraft to remain in the hands of those who have become strong enough to wield it through trail and exercise. It takes enormous dedication and perseverance to first take one's self out of the stagnant social strata of the modern world and then to literally seek to defy the human condition itself.

Above all, Witchcraft is a spontaneous art; the evocation, concentration and directing of power in alignment with the individual will of the Witch and Warlock. The most potent spells are conducted with the barest guidelines and this allows for one's true elemental connectivity to flow forth.

I am often asked about the work of the Coven and I have definite ideas concerning this. When a singleness of purpose can be agreed upon and a peak level of energy has been reached, a seasoned group can direct their power with staggering consequences. This situation however is more difficult to arrange that it may appear. People are conflicted, and witchcraft practitioners can sometimes be the most conflicted of all. But, if you get a group of witches together who can form a tight circle and really internally agree on their objectives, well then stand back.

An added benefit is the ability to expand the repertoire of the group workings through an advantage in numbers. Look at the group ritual work of the early Church of Satan. This still stands as a fantastic example of how intricate and powerful group work can be if conducted properly. Once again, the problem becomes people themselves. If you are lucky enough to have a few likeminded and devoted associates, then by all means take advantage of that. However, this book is primarily concerned with solitary Satanic Witchcraft and I shall leave the potential benefits of group work and ceremony to be discovered as part of your individual creative process.

For the modern Satanic Witch, Lesser Magic must begin with the erasing of the self as this self has been known and conceived of up until the point of termination. I am not advocating the denial of the self as some kind of dream or illusion as would various branches of eastern mysticism and I am certainly not proposing that the self is some small component mirror image ultimately contributing to the make-up of a deity or super-consciousness. These are obviously right handed seed beliefs and have no place in out black cosmology. What I am advocating is the witch's personal emphasis on the development of their Shadow. I will discuss the Witch's Shadow at length in a separate chapter.

As always, the Witch and Warlock step outside the confines of limited ideologies and primitive cosmologies in order to understand the "ego" as being entirely different from the "self" and even more removed from "self-importance." When I say we are engaged in erasing the self, what I really mean is that we have to start with the observation of human beings from a point of view devoid of heavy judgments and emotionally charged reactions to the world around us. The expert at Lesser Magic is one who has very intentionally situated themselves at the eye of the hurricane that is the human social realm. The sorcerer's "self" must be clear in order to most accurately reflect and understand that which is without, and to do this we must unlearn what we have come to take most for granted; our identity.

Within the pages of this modest yet potent book, you will find ritual, ceremonies and conjurations which exalt the powers of darkness and the force of life as it flows forth from the breath of Satan; the one and only matrix of nature supreme! Let not this work or any of the writings of the Dark Craft be misunderstood as resembling anything remotely religious, and let those who mistake authentic power for religion rot and perish when Baphomet's eyes find them cowering in the herd.

So, for those you who still have the fire and the force burning within; learn how to keep that rare and volatile essence alive. Hide it when prudent and focus its energies when necessary for the attainment of your indulgence, but be mindful of leaks. Today, more than ever Satanic Witches and Warlocks need to jealously guard the black flame within.

One crucial thing I believe a Satanist needs to understand in its totality is why they identify themselves as a Satanist. Intimately identifying with the archetype of individualism, liberty and rebellion should be a choice that I believe reflects a constant, rigorous personal self-examination and a deep understanding of what one wants out of life. For myself, Satanism is not part of a ready-made identity, but something I have grown into and within since I first read The Satanic Bible in high school detention at the age of fourteen. Not only does Satanism demand study over worship, but I personally believe Satanism demands work. Hard work and lots of it, which is of course counterbalanced by hard play. Satanism is important to me. I grew up during the satanic panic and distinctly remember my excitement when I would flick through the channels and discover real Satanists on an afternoon talk show, or when I would catch that rare glimpse of Anton LaVey or the Black House on some small news bit or occult documentary.

The Satanic Bible has become an important source of motivation, as well as a strategic guide that has aided me in shaping my own life in the most desirable of ways. I have had the opportunity to reread it twice during my recent deployments to hostile combat zones, and it has helped me to keep my mind clear, and my focus unwavering. Keeping this kind of mind set and attitude can be the difference between life and death. No exaggeration. I reflect on its contents on a daily basis, and find that even if I am unaware of it, I am putting the satanic principles therein to practical use. It really emphasizes my belief that life needs to be experienced and enjoyed in the here and now. I especially reflect on The Book of Satan most often, as I feel it helps to fuel the furnace that is my satanic will and resolve. I feel that The Satanic Bible is as applicable to society today, if not even more so, than it was when first introduced to the public. It seems to me that one of the main reasons this book has not changed since its publication is because its principles are fundamentally solid. The Satanic Bible has not needed to be rewritten or updated in order to keep up with the times. This says much in itself. Anton LaVey did not simply recognize the true carnal nature of humanity; he perpetually lived in a reality where the shadows of denied indulgence existed in the foreground of his perception.

In an age when human interaction was dependent on the use of superficial social niceties, Anton LaVey became a spokesperson for the grainy, dark and truthful world that coexists with that of the every day.

I can directly credit much of the success I have experienced in my outward professional life to the use of applied Satanic Witchcraft. I am a pragmatic Warlock, and if something does not work, no matter the allure, I quickly abandon it in favor of that which does. The practical application of certain concepts demands easily understandable examples. So, how has Satanism benefitted me? Certainly the most bountiful advantages I have experienced have been a direct result of my understanding of rational self-interest and in how I have learned to handle people. Responsibility to the responsible begins at home and as a Satanist I have no business complaining about that which I need not subject myself to. This eighth Rule of the Earth places full personal accountability on me as the center of my life and if I am unhappy with where I am or what is going on, the solution will originate where the problem did; with me.

Putting this satanic principle into daily practice has an immediate impact in one's affairs and continued implementation will have profound overreaching influence on the outcome of life events. It is also a core practice in Lesser Magic. Think about it; ordinary, average people do not consciously make an effort to not complain about their current state of affairs. The Witch knows this and gathers strength from self-immersion into and the adoption of qualities that are highly unique and border on non-human in character. As a matter of fact it has been my experience that most people complain most of the time about most things.

When I am seen by other to be one who does not complain about those things I need not subject myself to, it automatically sets me apart. I become a magical being that people want to be around and work alongside. The first two Satanic Rules of the Earth should be applied with the same frequency and intensity as the eighth, both being essential energy saving behaviors that will, when fully embodied, set one positively and noticeably apart from acquaintances and coworkers.

Another major touchstone of satanic wisdom has been the ruthless barring of individuals resembling anything akin to a psychic vampire from existing in my life. This state of affairs necessitates a constant predatory stance applied to the outside world, and again, if adhered to ruthlessly it insulates us from the vitality drainages so disregarded by those of a herd mentality. "Out there," as I like to call it, people tend to carelessly associate with whoever crosses their paths and this typically centers around one's occupational relations. Been there, done that! And through trial and error I, like most Satanists have developed a heightened degree of awareness when handling people.

So yes, Satanism benefits me every day and is absolutely central to who I am. It has played a tremendous part in getting me to the success I now claim, and will continue to play a part in getting me to where I am going.

Again, the true Satanic Witch and Warlock are the natural enemy of the herd animal that humanity has so willingly become. We delight in their downfall and revel in their misery and our magic is not only used for our own personal ends, but as part of a collective force that manifests and actively opposes all that is of human mediocrity. Man has had his chance, and he has failed.

We are living in the golden age of anonymity and I love it. Little did I know through my years of growing up and living in American society that I would eventually find such sheer delight in absolutely and totally erasing myself from the burden of a hum drum, ordinary existence and the tiresome social obligations that such an existence implies. It has been a process, and although I did not always really know exactly where I was headed and could not always see my grand objective as clearly as I would have liked, I know that I was headed in the right direction and one which most befitted my true animal nature.

Human social interaction has changed dramatically in only the last few decades, and even more since the era of the Victorian lady and gentleman. Where once one's social status was in a vital way detrimental to their physical well-being, nowadays it is a thing that we can mold and fabricate to suite whatever ends we feel necessary.

Now this is certainly not what I would call common knowledge, but it is true that in this age of anonymity, the person we present to the world of human social intercourse has become less a culmination of historical forces acting to shape the individual psyche and more a façade personally tailored to achieve a series of given ends. "Many, if not most, of the people we encounter each day don't know who we are and will never find out. Even our acquaintances may be fleeting. People move often, change jobs often. So a reputation for integrity matters less now, and sacrifices of all kinds – even for colleagues or neighbors – are less likely to be repaid in the future. These days an upper-middle-class man who by example teaches his son to be slick and superficially sincere, to tell minor lies in profusion, to work harder on promise than delivery, may well be equipping him for success" (Wright, 1994.)

This freedom from the development of real integrity of character has without a doubt led to the creation of masses of the most shallow, uninteresting and uncreative human drones the earth has ever witnessed. This, while probably an evolutionary tragedy, suites me fine. When I was an angst-ridden teenager, I resented, with every hormone saturated fiber of my being, the hazy status-quo which my parents and those allied with them were trying to perpetuate and preserve. I knew their world was a dying one, but I had no idea that the conflict of interests between their generation and mine would eventually yield an environment that was to be perfect. Perfect, for certain individuals of a unique and strong character; perfect for the Satanic Witch.

The homogenous landscape of America is the ideal hunting ground for those of us who know best how to utilize an appearance of mediocrity. Who I am is an illusion, crafted by my desire and presented in a manner that best suites my purposes at any given time. I have the Master's diploma on the wall to show and demonstrate how I worked so hard and actually took part in the farce that modern education has become. I have the respectable "career," which gives me an abundance of automatic credibility with any audience. I have the very nice two story suburban home with the exquisitely green lawn in which I can leave the world behind and pursue my devilish delights.

Who I really am is irrelevant, and the energy that I save through my non-engagement with people leaves me invigorated and able to focus my desire wherever I may. I have no social obligations beyond those genuine relationships I hold most dear, and this self-created condition has fostered a kind of freedom I never thought possible.

No one cares where I go, what my religion is or if I believe in UFOs. People are too wonderfully immersed in their own daily concerns to think that I could possibly be any kind of threat. They have their pithy self-absorptions, mostly concerning getting ahead at work, which "selfie" to post or who is screwing who and are too focused on second-hand obsessions to be interested in anyone outside their immediate cozy circle.

Things were not always like this. I remember as a young adult how daring and actually dangerous it was to appear different than those around you. People cared what kind of music you listened too, what kinds of books you read, and most importantly, how you physically appeared. This focus has generally disappeared in American society, and a status quo has been born which keeps people subdued and unconcerned for that which does not interfere with their comfort. Bread and games for the people, and this allows those of us who seek out more obscure paths to self-satisfaction the freedom to move through the night unnoticed and unmolested.

Internalizing an understanding of how witchcraft works is primarily a solitary endeavor. I personally have a fairly cynical view of group interaction. There is always an agenda on the part of human beings. If an occult group does not have a very clearly defined purpose it most often degenerates into a mess of competing egos and sexual escapades. In the past when I was affiliated with occult groups it was simply because there were really limited avenues for learning and seeking out others of like mind.

The creation of our personal night side realm begins with the understanding that such an avenue of activity and existence can be molded to suit our desire and purposes. We begin with the expansion of ideas and the formation of agreements, or new perceptual contracts made with ourselves and one another as witches.

A critical examination of our native socialization is crucial in being able to truly assess our effectiveness in solidifying such contracts. The next step is practical action. We begin to act upon these new fundamental ideas, thus generating the energetic movement of thought in a specific direction.

Our thoughts and actions combine with the thoughts and actions of each other, and so an entire socio-perceptual consensus is brought into being. This begins by simply challenging the known constraints of our culture and selectively putting forth an effort to countermand the energy that we have already put into motion by accepting our role. We take one major aspect of how most human beings, including ourselves currently live in the western world, and we choose to challenge that way with other behaviors that are diametrically opposed.

The psychic vampires are everywhere, and not only that but they have transcended many past limitations to become entire conglomerates of energy draining entities devoted to your destruction. Choose each and every battle carefully and retreat into the night, where we belong to replenish and revitalize. The war never ends, but does indeed become more insidious.

Some witches avoid the herd altogether and enjoy the benefits of a solitary life, either by the circumstances they have created through their efforts, or through naturally occurring series of life events which have led them to a place where the daily banter of the world is easily shut out or has been forsaken altogether.

I however am not one among these few. This is not altogether by choice because if I could I would for the most part certainly pursue the life of a solitary warlock. It is rather by the designs of my inner intent, as is continuously indicated by the nature of my dreams as well as the outer life situations and conditions that regularly present themselves to me. The time for solitary work may very well be in the distant future, but at this time I am called to find the challenges necessary for my growth within the arena of modern human beings.

At first thought moving among the herd may appear to be a very disadvantageous position for a warlock to be in, but it has recently dawned on me that only within the noise of the daily world can one truly hear the absolute silence behind the chatter, and only by confronting the behavior of our fellow human beings can one's impeccability be exercised to the point where our link with the abstract becomes enlivened, clear and functional. A Satanic Witch cannot hope to make any progress in a vacuum, unchallenged and subsequently undeveloped in their strength and skill.

Now, a brief word concerning the current nuisance known as the "Satanic Temple." While I can find it within myself to respect a witch's or warlock's misguided alignment with the TST, I simply have no interest in the organization's position. I took a cursory skim of the TST web site a while back and I have read Magus Peter Gilmore's written responses on the Church of Satan's position regarding the TST. I agree with these views on a personal level, mostly because I am not a social activist and I simply don't care about personally championing the cause of religious secularism by forcing the Christian majority to acknowledge my Baphomet medallion. "While the members of the Church of Satan are secularists, not every Satanist considers the public displays of various religions to be offensive or worth combatting." This definitely applies to me. I actually enjoy the natural polarity that exists between the spiritual "white light" religions and the one that I have thoughtfully chosen. I am a Satanist in the true I-theistic sense of the word and I choose to spend my time pursuing my own projects, relationship, career, enjoyments, etc. Yes, I have been much more open about being a Satanist over the past year and this too reflects a personal choice and approach to my life in general. I read the Satanic Bible in detention when I was fourteen years old, so I'm a bit of an old schooler here, and my attachment to the Church of Satan and the philosophy of Satanism as created by Anton LaVey are tied to very deep personal history with me. I really don't know how much "angst" exists between the Church of Satan and the Satanic Temple other than what I see on Facebook, and I really don't care. Magus Gilmore and High Priestess Nadramia have not asked anyone to champion the Church of Satan and actively denounce the Satanic Temple, and this is good because it would not only be a major turn off for me, but I have no interest in doing so. Also, I don't consider the Church of Satan a "sect" as it is the "first above-ground organization in history openly dedicated to the acceptance of Man's true nature—that of a carnal beast, living in a cosmos that is indifferent to our existence." This is a fact.

Not only have I met both Magus Gilmore and High Priestess Nadramia and found them to be of superior intelligence and simply wonderful company, I am also happy, content and impressed with how they continue to maintain and guard the integrity of the Church of Satan and Satanism over 50 years after the founding of the Church of Satan. This, in itself is a feat worthy of praise knowing how people generally exploit anything that they can soon after the passing of a religion's founder. I really don't know what people expect from our High Priest and High Priestess other than the decisive, perfect articulation of what Satanism is and public representation of the organization of non-joiners known as the Church of Satan.

On a final note, I aggressively recommend Anton LaVey's essay from "Satan Speaks" entitle "how to be a Sorcerer." If you are truly interested in how to understand satanic witchcraft you will give it a read.

"The real satanist is not quite so easily recognized as such"

— Anton Szandor LaVey, The Satanic Bible

~2~

The Witch's Shadow

Matthew Hopkins Witch Finder Generall
My Imps names are
Holt
1 Ilemauzar
2 Pyewackett
Jarmara
Sacke & Sugar
3 Pecke in the Crowne
4 Griezzell Greedigutt
Newes
Vinegar tom

Within the realm of our perceptual possibilities, there is a power disconnected from that which we consider to be our predictable, linear self. Our every-day socialized persona is a paper-thin, weak construct formed through our acceptance and enactment of the dictums that originate in the social order, but the being that truly animates us is a force that can be systematically strengthened and made aware of itself through Dreaming.

Every Witch is born a Witch and although we each may go through decades of turmoil and struggle in the human realm of mediocrity, there is a part of us that will remain alive and active; a part that cannot be silenced or extinguished. This is also the part of the witch that originates in the unknown of the night and in Dreaming and if it is groomed and fed it will become strong, eventually ascending as the dominant aspect of the Witch or Warlock themselves.

This is the twin self, the Dreaming Double, or what we shall call from here on, the Witch's Shadow. The Shadow is not the "soul." It is something every human being has, but that only witch's feel as a central and fundamental part of themselves. Only witch's strengthen their shadow, and this is done first through acknowledgement of its existence and then through use. Once again, we are talking about the magic of attention and perception. How many of us have had dreams of events that have come true to greater or lesser extent?

The Witch's Shadow personifies and echoes nature itself, and treats, in a most independent manner those unfortunate enough to cross the witch as nothing more than prey in a simple, predatory universe. Being of clear mind and high intellect, the Satanic Witch understands that witchcraft is their own privileged prerogative, developed through years of discipline and hardship, to be used judiciously and purposefully in the battle that is survival.

Those capable of destroying their enemies without incurring unnecessary harm to themselves are, without a doubt of superior mind and skill. The Satanic Witch does not waste untold energy and time morally deliberating about whether or not a particular target deserves their wrath.

The Witch's Shadow as the dreaming self is the part of us that is utterly connected to the cosmos as a field of energy; it receives the deepest impulses from the raw energy of nature and translates these impulses into symbolic imagery. This is the language of dreams and the witch is so very different from the ordinary person precisely because this natural connection is so strong it generates a force that seemingly acts independently of the witch's physical self. If you have ever asked yourself the question, "am I a witch?" then you can be assured that if you understand the above explanation, the answer is a definite yes!

Once we understand what the Witch's Shadow is in the best way we can comprehend it, then we must begin to bring it closer to our waking consciousness and strengthen it. This is done by first becoming more active with our dreams and then we move on to reinforcing it through the use of ceremonies and the enactment of spell work.

There is no room for dogma in true witchcraft. Dogma is not a creative process and thus it is really in essence the opposite of witchcraft. Dogma is only used to help adhere to the most basic structural components of ceremonial work. While many ceremonial workings will benefit from structure, a ritual may contain impulsive additions where individual interpretation and inspiration may occur. With time and experience, the adherence to dogma and structure will be almost entirely replaced with greater forms of innovative expression.

The social facet of perception tells us what we are, what is important in the world and what we should not bother paying attention to. We are removed from the naturally occurring universe primarily because we disregard anything that does not have social value, or personal applicability. That which has social value and personal applicability is immediately gratifying to us as persons and we automatically follow the path laid out for us; a path that continually enhances our sense of self through a manufactured series of stimuli that either satisfy or repel.

The primary and crucial task of the witch is to know the social description of the world for what it is and to begin methodically separating this description from what can truly be perceived and understood. This is an overwhelming task as our socialization is the only means we are familiar with for interacting with the world around us. This being recognized, we do not want to entirely disable our capability of intelligent interaction, but we do wish to develop the proficiency of isolating the social description of a phenomenon and intentionally relating to it in more sophisticated ways.

We begin with a rudimentary set of premises that concern the fundamental nature of the material world in which we all operate. First, we regard perception as the root of subjective existence and the interplay of our physical senses with those energy fields at large that make up the world in which we find ourselves. The witch and warlock seek to be continuously aware that there are two fields of awareness within our immediate grasp. There are configurations of energy which we transform into physical data through our five senses, and there is, on top of that a social description which we have been taught to impose upon those things we have learned to perceive. This social aspect of perception is an inheritance. It is passed down to us by our ancestors, and it is modified according to the needs of these people at particular periods in time.

Without this shared description, the world would lack meaning and we would have no way to interact as a species. All of our ideas about the world and the way that it works have been conditioned by the tenets and rules of our social description. Our most inner notions and beliefs have grown out of this ancestral heirloom, and we are taught, out of our instinctual avoidance of the unknown, to avoid questioning it.

My central objective in writing this book is to challenge the Satanic Witch and Warlock to take action and live the principles that will lead to power. It is easy to wear black clothing, buy books and say you love Satan. Anyone can do that, but it is far more challenging and rewarding to walk the Left Hand Path as a matter of conviction, eschewing the herd lifestyle and mentality and acting as a force of opposition in this world. There is a garbage heap of books out there at this time that seem to be Left Hand Path texts, but upon closer examination they are little more than white light manuals covered over in black cloth with diabolical looking cover stamps. Some have merit but the Left Hand Path is a sound philosophical approach which is definable by precise terminology and Black Magic is a discipline that is an extension of this.

I hear many practitioners who seem to be confused in their terminology and deem themselves as Left Hand Path adherents but rely on concepts like transcendence or ascent.

Whether one considers themselves to be a "theistic" Satanist or not, the Left Hand Path is still the way of the earth and the glorification of the self through a very rigorous process.

You can call this process initiation or ascent if you want, but I personally avoid terminology that takes power away from the Satanist themselves in favor of a "higher" ideal that has not been self-defined. The only things I want to transcend are my own limitations and those placed on me as a social participant in the modern world. Many of these concepts reek of early gnostic Christianity, so I think it's important for practitioners to really think about what is being offered by writers, including myself.

Witchcraft is power that is focused and directed by the mind of the practitioner. The success of any spell is contingent upon the strength and control of the witch's awareness, shadow, emotional focus and their skill in sensing and directing energy.

Understanding energy, discriminating between dissimilar energies, and directing energy is the basis of all witchcraft. This control comes through USE. How thoroughly and regularly we apply ourselves to a commitment to live our power will determine how powerful one's works are. Newly awakened witches are encouraged to begin slow and with the elementary goal of connecting with their power. Some among us are born with a natural capacity to gather power faster than others, but this is no matter as long as we never quit.

The Witch's Shadow does not have the ability to reason. Energy takes the route of least opposition, unless it is properly encoded and directed. For example, many of us desire additional income. The witch does not simply insist "Cash is approaching to me." If your power is not directed properly, this intent could possibly manifest at a temporary job where you regularly handle money, like a treasurer for example, or somehow through your standard paycheck. These are the avenues of least resistance. You must affirm "Great quantities of unrestricted and easy cash is approaching me. This currency is entirely mine to possess and use as I desire." You would furthermore affirm the money come in a constructive way. You don't want a loved one to pass away or leave you an inheritance or acquire the currency in a way that would be disagreeable.

Declarations should be repeated with intent, over and over in your mind with the understanding that your Witch's Shadow is listening, understands and will respond.

Another vital point of interest is that the Witch's Shadow runs on a very specific kind of fuel; sexual energy. Indiscriminately wasted sexual energy equates to a weak shadow and thus a weak, inefficient witch. Women and men are vastly different from one another and this is reflected in how their sexual energy flows, is stored, released and directed. Witches have a sexual energetic cycle that corresponds to their reproductive/menstrual cycle and the phases of the moon. Warlocks are all about build up and release, so all in all, witches have the advantage as males must carefully save their sexual energy and start a new build up each time it is released. Now, it must also be admitted that every individual is different with different levels of sexual energy to begin with and biological age is also a factor. Some may be able to build up and expend their energy in greater frequency that others. All females really need to do is capitalize on their natural energetic cycle as it is a direct connection they have with the cosmos and it is a female's privilege to plug into it at any time.

"Sexual release for the sole purpose of pleasure and bodily excitation should take place specifically on nine nights of the yearly cycle. These occasions should be well planned debaucheries devoted to the dark powers, self-deification and unrestrained lust. They should resemble the traditional witches' Sabbath and may even center on the work of a traditional satanic coven and the strengthening of that coven's chosen dark egregore. Four main Sabbats should be observed on Samhain or the night of October 31st and into the darkness of November 1st, on Candlemass which is the night of February 1st into the darkness of March 1st, again on Walpurgis which is the night of April 30th and finally on Lammas which is on the night of July 31st. These ceremonial revelries may be structured in any way that excites and stimulates and they are best conducted in privacy and isolation away from the judging and prying eyes of the herd. The complete exhaustion of the senses is the objective of these events, devoted ultimately to personal pleasure and the glorification of darkness over that of light. Multiple participants are recommended as are all the trappings of a good Saturnalia celebration.

The four lesser revelries should take place on the night of December 22nd, March 22nd, June

22nd and September 22nd. These minor Sabbats correspond roughly with the estbats of the yearly cycle and should more properly be devoted to lesser celebrations and works of dark sorcery. These are ideal times for personal or group workings of a wholly materialistic nature perhaps followed by celebrations of the flesh and senses. The abstract sorcery objective here is both the experience of extreme forms of indulgence and the nurturing on non-ordinary appetites as well as the energetic clearing out of one's energetic tensions that have built up through the use of the dark formulas throughout the yearly lunar phases. The last night of ecstasy should be on the night of one's day of birth. "

Satanism is a religion of the physical realm and the individual's mind. While identifying as a Satanic Witch or Warlock is not necessary to be a Satanist, I would guess that most Satanists have become proficient in or at least have taken a thoughtful interest in witchcraft and occult. Witchcraft has always been equal to Satanism and in turn, secrecy. There can be unparalleled excitement for the witch in appearing to the outside world as an average person, while harboring a satanic altar in one's home and the dark power of satanic witchcraft in one's heart.

Witchcraft can be thought of as the path rare individuals sometimes take in an attempt to attain the inherent and natural powers of the mind that are our true legacy. Christianity and their theistic brethren have always done all they can to discourage and scare average people away from endeavoring to use the natural power which we Satanic Witches and Warlocks have unlimited access to. The singular intention of Christianity as a world view has forever been to eradicate all real creativity and carnal satisfaction, thus preventing the human race from opening the powers of the mind and body in order to keep power in the hands of a few. Civilization has been held treacherously and intentionally back by all theistic religions, particularly Christianity.

I have adopted Anton LaVey's assertion that one's birthday is the most important high holiday of the year as is in keeping with the self-centric nature of the Left Hand Path in general. I personally set aside this day for enjoyments of a strictly personal nature followed by a night of carnal realization all devoted towards mine own self as an expression of willed self-creation. This is a night to indulge and revel in one's achievements." *(The Infernal Path, Dark Harvest, 2013).*

With enough repeated intent and enough energy, the Witch's Shadow will respond in truly unbelievable, unpredictable ways. The witch's dreams will inevitably provide a window into the Shadow's activity and I must recommend the Witch and Warlock keep a detailed dream journal because simply focusing one's attention on the activities of the Witch's Shadow strengthens our link with it and gives us a greater capacity to remember our dreams.

CONSTANTLY REMEMBER THAT ENERGY TAKES THE PATH OF LEAST OPPOSITION AND IT DOES NOT HAVE THE CAPACITY TO REASON!

-4-

Elemental Force

The Witches and Warlocks of the dark path draw their strength from the energy of the earth and their deepest animal nature. It is my firm understanding wrought through experience that the power of magic is bio-energetic in nature. This does not necessarily mean that sexual energy and the release of power through orgasm is the only means of performing acts of witchcraft however, sexual energy it certainly the easiest, quickest and most potent form of bio-energy available for the satanic witch and warlock.

Satanic witches are of course inherently different from warlocks when it comes to building up and wielding the power of magic. Females are simply built differently than males and their power is immense for this reason; it is also why witches really do not require the build-up and conservation of energy the way the warlock does. Chinese medicine and various martial arts based practices assert that women only lose the majority of their base bio-energy through giving birth to children and to a much lesser degree, through monthly menstruation. A male is understood to lose their life force primarily through orgasm. In this view, females are the sustaining, passive and creative base of human existence while males are the inflammatory, driving and forceful impulse towards the disruption which allows for the conditions of change.

As I have experimented over the years with my own sexual energy with these general ideas in mind and through my observation of others, I have come to the definite conclusion that magic should be approached and worked in entirely different ways for the witch and warlock, particularly sex magic and the use or orgasm in sorcery.

As I am a male of the species, let me begin with what I have discovered as the best approach to witchcraft for the warlock. Sexual bio-energy is the physical foundation for everything a warlock does, and as such it needs to be accumulated, stored and released with great consideration and with discrimination. A witch's energy level fluctuates with their monthly bio-lunar cycle, while a warlock is all build-up and release. Have you ever noticed how absolutely amorous, ethereal and stunning a woman is during the ovulation period of her monthly phase? I have known many witches to flat out admit that a few weeks before they get their period, while they are ovulating, their power of seduction and sexual desire peaks tremendously.

The warlock is not built to nourish and grow a child within their body, but to seek out, fertilize and then defend the mother of their future offspring. There is of course an emotional component to all of this tumultuous sexual insanity and this ensures that both parents will play a role in the upbringing and protection of their young.

The warlock is all build-up and release and for this reason conserving and intelligently directing one's sexual energy will immediately be seen to improve magical ability and overall worldly influence. According to Chinese medicine, the majority of our energy (Jing) is produced in the kidneys. In males it is stored in the semen and when semen is not expended through unnecessary ejaculation, it is refined by the body and re-absorbed.

There is some scanty recent scientific research on the development of sperm and the orgasm in males and I have certainly taken these somewhat shady findings into consideration, but nothing can stand in for true experimentation conducted by you within the arena of your worldly life. What I have found is that avoiding masturbation and allowing the steady growth of my arousal to increase has a tremendous impact on my daily vitality, confidence and interaction with people, especially women. It also allows for a long buildup of intent and desire toward a chosen magical goal, which when finally released ritually during orgasm, has a far greater impact. Of course, I don't expect anyone to just take my word for it. Do your own research and find out how best to harness and apply your own bio-energy. There is plenty of material out there on Chinese longevity practices and the recent "NoFap" movement has spawned a wealth of informative videos from a variety of abstainers and practitioners.

By no means am I advocating the denial of sex or even orgasm as a kind of aesthetic, mystical practice; I am simply pointing out the power of sexual energy and the role it can potentially play in the individual witch's or warlock's quest.

The witch will have an entirely different orientation towards sexual energy and it will primarily involve capitalizing on their own bio-energetic monthly cycle. Again, according to Chinese energy workers, females can have all the orgasms they wish because they are not energetically depleted in this way however, child bearing needs to be kept in mind as it pertains to the exhaustion of the witch's life force. I am not a female and I am simply passing on the most general information from the research I have done, so if this is distasteful to you, I apologize and implore you to do your own investigation.

I also mentioned that females loose a bit of their base "jing" through monthly menstruation, but just as the warlock may conserve their energy through non-ejaculation, the witch has alternatives as well. I knew of one incredibly powerful witch who would take "blood baths" during the heaviest days of her period. She would concoct an herbal bath with various plants having lunar correspondences and then draw luke-warm water into which she would immerse herself and allow her blood to flow. As she soaked, she would focus on drawing all the energy from her blood back into her body, visualizing her increased radiance and youthfulness.

I have come to liken acts of witchcraft as being operationally similar to what one experiences when attempting to remember some tidbit of information once known, but forgotten over a significant period of time. This is basically, in my experience and understanding how magic (particularly sex magic) works. First, there is a desire to recall the name, song, place, product or whatever. Then, once the desire to remember is frustrated (sexual build-up and tension) by initial failure, more effort is devoted to the remembering process (continued intention). If the desired information cannot be brought back into present recall in a timely manner (limitations of the material world) and sufficient energy has been expended in the determination to recollect, the affair is typically forgotten out of frustration or in favor or more stimulating thoughts and experiences (the release of orgasm). Usually, after some time has passed and we have moved wholly on to new things; pop! The original nugget of trivia enters unexpectedly into our conscious and we have attained our original desire to remember the object of our intent (objective achieved through the release of energy after prolonged desire, visualization and finally detachment). I have come to understand that successful acts of magic parallel this progression and that there are three critical stages in any operation with conditions which must be satisfactorily met if we are to experience fruition in our work.

The first stage concerns the origination and formation of the desire itself. Unsuccessful endeavors, broken lives and the chronically stagnate are all hallmarks of conflicted desire and lack of self-knowledge. Not knowing what one truthfully wants is a paralyzing condition that leaves people open to the insidious sway of contemporary commercialism. Stated simply; if you don't know what you want out of life, there are an ever present multitude of influences masquerading as options that will magically step in and shape your desires and choices for you. We are all consumers to some degree, however there is a point where self-awareness distinguishes those whose identity is calcified around being plugged into the world as a consumer and those who wholeheartedly reject this role and assume the mantle of the "other." These are the self-definers, the creators and self-actualizers. These are the Satanists, and to be in this state pre-necessitates an absence of inner conflict, and such a condition itself is a prerequisite of the ability to perform magic. Average, ordinary people cannot work magic because they approach every endeavor from this initial state of conflict. To "know thyself" is not only an ageless maxim of wisdom, it is a detrimental requirement for the aspiring witch and warlock.

Along with the proper understanding and formation of the desired attainment comes the necessity to fully grasp the implications of the "balance factor." This means that we have achieved an accurate understanding of how achievable our desire is in relation to the means available for accomplishing its attainment.

Some things are easily achieved and can be had by saying the right few words and knowing the right people, however most of us have desires that are far more involved and complex in their origin and span of influence. Wanting a Master's degree in business administration is a specific, yet complex desire that necessitates a numerous series of operation on several different levels in order for its fulfillment to be individually realized. The more moving parts an idealized desire has, the greater will be the need to invest varying degrees of personal energy in the form of time and attention.

The art of applying the balance factor is the faculty of being adept in reducing the steps necessary for the attainment of a goal. Pushing down a wall in order to squash a mosquito is an analogy which humorously points out the opposite of the successful application of the balance factor and give us a kind of gauge in what behaviors and thoughts should be avoided.

With this very general but important discussion concerning our basic sexual power in mind, I would like to move onto my conception of the witch's and warlock's elemental root powers and how they may be identified and tapped into for use.

Beginning from the metaphysical orientation that asserts human beings are each composed of both male and female energy, I have found it extremely beneficial to assign the primary characteristics of the four traditional "elements" to the natural expressive and fundamental power of each individual witch and warlock.

In Chinese martial arts and energy work, the human body contains three important, primary energy centers that are somewhat like batteries. They are called the three dantians. Viewed as the main energy storage facilities in the human body, all we comprehend about our physicality, emotive balance, and link to intuition can be ascribed to the condition of these three energetic chakra-like centers.

The three dantians:

1. The lower - Situated behind the naval encompassing your lower bowl area.

2. The middle - Situated in your chest where the physical heart is located.

3. The upper - Situated behind the forehead where the physical brain is located.

I need not go into the complexities of these energy centers, but for my purposes here I will simply explain that each one of these energy storehouses is constructed of female and male energy and that in Chinese energy work this is depicted as the traditional Ying and Yang symbol. I have found that the four traditional elements fit perfectly into this conception and allow us to identify the witch's and warlock's root elemental power based on the degree and balance of female/male energy and how this energy expresses itself in each of us individually.

Each of us can be thought to have a primary active element and a primary passive element. These elements are the earthly powers we have an affinity for and can tap into and channel in the most natural manner. This is my own working conception and just a simple way I get my creative energy going before and during my own workings.

My own primary element is air, and it is an active one. I have a root affinity with air for a multitude of reasons and when I work witchcraft it is this element that I tap into. I often will open up all the windows of my home on a chilly autumn night and allow the cold wind to swirl around my working space, feeling the power of my witchcraft connecting with the greater natural power of the air as the candles violently flicker and shadows dance about the room. As I close the working, I feel my intent carried away on the wind and within the in the smoke of my chosen incense to become manifest in the material world or to take seed in the minds of those target individuals who quietly slumber.

My passive primary element is water and I directly connect with this force of nature for a variety of purposes, but particularly for energetic renewal, self-cleansing, and sexual gratification and even to cause storms and problematic weather.

The Satanic Witches' creative power is expressed on a regular basis through their own personal fulfillment. This is something that is hypocritically denied by the herd of humanity and all mystically based esoteric schools who are basically committed to spreading dogma and stagnant ritual performance. The satanic witch and warlock use the destruction, lust and compassion ritual framework to conduct most magical operations as these fundamental categories were understood by Anton LaVey to capture almost all of the individual's possible concerns and desires. I have personally added wealth and material fulfillment as a distinct category of its own and I conveniently allocate destruction, lust, compassion and wealth witchcraft to the elements of air, fire, water and earth. Of course one's individual creativity needs to play the primary role in all workings and we should take these basic ideas many stages further, using modifications and adaptations which shall personalize the ritual process to the desires of the individual witch.

Destruction Witchcraft - Element of air, the image of the tornado descending and tearing all to shreds. Ruled by Lucifer whose power causes the bare truth of reality to sine through when all has been cleared away by the power of the wind. I personally use the image of a black Baphomet on a Halloween orange background for workings of destruction.

Lust Witchcraft - Element of fire, the image of twisting naked bodies encircling the central witch-fire of the high black mass. Ruled by Satan in his form of the black goat of the woods. I use the image of Baphomet with reds and purples for works of lust and romance.

Compassion Witchcraft - Element of water, the image of the healthy human fetus growing in the dark, watery womb. Ruled by the great serpent Leviathan of the deep. I use the image of an ocean blue Baphomet on a field of midnight blue encircled by a serpent.

Wealth Witchcraft – Element of earth, the image of solid gold veins embedded and running through the entire planet. Ruled by the devil Mammon, lord of excessive wealth and personal gain. I use the image of a vibrant green Baphomet on a black background encircled by dollar signs.

The Infernal Elemental Energies

Fire Witchcraft – Employed through invoking and directing the fire element. Fire witchcraft comprises:

Sexual prowess and energy, destruction, confidence, fame, success in material pursuits, pleasure, securing, charisma, increasing health and vitality, healing, major sudden changes, adaptability, attraction, stimulation, enthusiasm, creativity, energy, gaining control, changing luck, causing justice to occur, protection, success, magical power, creativity, enthusiasm, energy, stamina, revenge, anger, pure sexual lust, and physical gratification, courage, determination, dealing with enemies. Provoking accidents, fires, injuries, athletics and strength. Used to cause lust, generate energy, strength, sexual energy, dynamism, passionate love, physical desire, courage, will power, and any kind of competition. Excellent energy to increase self-empowerment before workings of the darkest witchcraft operation. When utilized for these workings, fire can be used to cause unexpected attacks, misfortunes, bloodshed, violence, and animosity. Fire can also be used to provoke wars, lawlessness, and brutality.

Air Witchcraft – Employed through invoking and directing the air element. Air witchcraft comprises:

The powers of discord directed at the enemy, intellectual prowess, communication, audio media, and literature. Improving concentration, mental power, learning ability, speech, writing, publishing, media, gossip, slander, job interviews, rumors, verbal communication, motivational speaking/influencing others through the power of your voice and words. Air witchcraft also stimulates misunderstanding, confusion, bad temper, anxiety, nervous fatigue, quarrels, and general discord.

Water Witchcraft – Water witchcraft is employed through invoking the elemental properties of the water element. Primarily lends its power to all forms of rejuvenation, healing, creation sorcery, sex witchcraft and any magic where bodily fluids are utilized. Sex witchcraft can be combined with the other primary elements as well, but is governed by the water element.

Youth witchcraft, friendships and strong emotional bonds, physical attraction and charms to cause fascination, witchcraft to cause invisibility or change appearances, marital harmony, social gatherings, indulgence of food and drink and general pleasure. Increasing psychic ability, telepathy, mind reading, the Art of Dreaming, communication, absorbing knowledge intuitively. Excellent for the initiation of new beginnings and growth. Protecting the homestead. Provoking jealousy, greediness, distrust, resentment, illness, infection, and unrest. Water witchcraft, when directed at an enemy target can cause them to be exceedingly emotional, have violent reactions and having a very problematic time with being calm and objective.

Earth Witchcraft – Employed through invoking and directing the darkest aspects of the earth element and includes:

Money and all forms of material gain, fertility, abundance, physical healing, communication with shadow entities, increase in all its forms, possessions, physical indulgence and material pleasure. Earth witchcraft is utilized in death magic and can be used along with all death related energy. Also always employed in any form of binding and to absorb the enemy's attention and obscure reality.

Again, as witchcraft is the spontaneous art of applying focus and power to a given end, most of your true workings will be spur of the moment and quite often as a result of some immediate situation that presents itself.

I used to live in a rather crowded European city and my thick, frosted glass door opened directly to a busy street. One summer evening I was sitting quietly on my couch reading, when I heard a few males talking right outside my door on the street. I intuitively felt the arrogance and aggression in one of their voices and I distinctly hear the word for American in their language. This perked my interest considerably, so I peeked out from my shadowed interior through the small slats of my open window to get a good view of the men. They were gathered around a small blue car which evidently belonged to one of them and they began to play some euro-crap dance music at an excessive volume. Just as my anger was beginning to rise, one of them turned a spat a sizable wad of mucous and spittle on my glass front door. Perfect, I thought to myself. I relaxed and returned to my reading until the unruly group of morons became bored and left.

When the darkness approached, I opened my front door, took a slightly dampened paper tissue and mopped up the partially dried spittle the moron had left behind. I then allowed the tissue to dry out in the heat of the night.

The following evening, with disgust and contempt in my heart, I lit a small incense coal, called to the Prince of the Powers of the Air and his devils and slowly roasted the tissue on the hot coal. The smoke wafted malignantly out my window as I whispered curses and beseeched my infernal allies to torment the spitter in the most appropriate manner.

I later went to bed and was woken up by the sound of a tremendous boom and the screeching of car wheels on the street in front of my home. I jumped out of bed, ran to the window and to my sheer delight, beheld the spitter's little blue car had been severely smashed by another vehicle that had taken the corner to the right of my building excessively fast. The vehicle that had hit the spitter's blue car drove away immediately, leaving the blue car with disabling damage to the entire rear right side.

Needless to say, I was beyond delighted and as a bonus I got to see the spitter's wrecked car sit directly in front of my house for months before he could have it removed. I lit my black candles and plenty of incense in recognition of the mercurial powers of the air that had heard my call and responded so quickly with such force.

The Satanic Altar

The Satanic altar is a magical commonality found among almost all Satanic Witches and Warlocks and no matter what one chooses to use as a place of power, it always represents the manifestation of the infernal powers and elements on the material plane; a witch's and warlock's true area of activity.

The satanic alter should be a relatively balanced affair. I personally find that simplicity yields the greatest results and that neatness in this area counts. Also, a nice tidy altar is so much easier to clean and rearrange when the need arises. Every item you choose to place on this space should have definite purpose and meaning. I will not list the most commonly employed satanic altar accoutrements here as I plan on expanding on this in a forthcoming work that will not only serve as a deeper discussion concerning the satanic ritual chamber, but also be a satanic ritual and spell book containing my own unique workings. The true inventiveness of satanic genius cannot be stifled by rigid thinking and standardization. Since our animal senses have such potential for experience and expression, a dogmatic, sterile collection of writings on the subject is counterproductive to our purposes.

Remember, a true witch strives to increase their power for personal benefit and the preservation of the earth that sustains us. If you find yourself stagnating and your mind being clouded by the heavy pull of the energy of modern times and all the superficiality that implies, then break away immediately and find solitude and in this solitude begin to employ your witchcraft again until you are strengthened and can go back out among the herd.

Use witchcraft every day! Let it breathe through you and manifest in even the smallest of your acts.

-4-

The Witch's Arsenal

I was born a Witch and knew this from a very early age. Not only was I the typical "oddball" as a child, but I also felt a strong living connection to a strange "force" from my earliest days. I believe each of us experiences various external factors in our childhood that can hinder, warp or quicken our innate power and I was certainly no exception to this. I was fortunate in some ways during my very early childhood as I was generally left alone and anything that may have been seen as strange about my behavior was dismissed as part of the shifting formative nature of my age at that time.

It took me decades of struggle and personal anguish before I could simply accept myself in a total way. One of my earliest recollections regarding my nature occurred when I was five years old. I was a very troubled sleeper as a child and among the many difficulties I had, falling out of my bed was top among them. My parents had even installed brackets on the sides of my bed to keep me in it while I slept. I remember very clearly one night while my parents were downstairs in our home entertaining some friends, I woke suddenly and found myself looking down at my bed from about eight feet in the air. At first I obviously thought I was dreaming and was quite disoriented, however upon coming to my full senses, I knew that I was actually floating above my bed, suspended in the air. This only lasted a second and as my child's mind pondered on the strangeness of this phenomenon, I suddenly felt my body's mass and I plummeted down and crashed with a very loud thud into my bed.

My parents and their friends rushed upstairs, alarmed by the noise and fully expecting me to be on the floor. I think everyone was a bit confused to see me still laying in my bed and simply assumed that I had fallen out of it and immediately gotten back up. For years as I "grew up" I dismissed this experience as some kind of lucid dream, particularly because I was an avid lucid dreamer as a child, however now I know better.

As a child growing up in a world where mediocrity meant respectability, I was eventually marginalized by family and peers as I struggled to assimilate myself within the ranks of the supernormal. This kind of unnatural stifling of one's natural tendencies is bound to distort a person's growth process, and while I did eventually emerge victorious, it has not been without experiencing decades of internal and external struggle. Many of the sensitive among us bear our unique battle scars.

In the modern world, those who have been born with one foot set within the netherworld are most often relegated to the domain of the discarded among humanity. We are considered strange at best and outright freaks of nature at the worst. The current popular interest in the paranormal, particularly hauntings and mediumship can be seen in a broader historical sense as part of a recurring cycle of trends that surface now and again among the masses as a result of that indescribable, profound and subtle connection each person has to the dead and the vastness of the unknown in general. Many are naturally drawn to these subjects in their search for meaning and as a way of coming to terms with the chord that is ceaselessly resonating inside each one of us, reminding us of our eternal connection to nature.

While witchcraft is powered through the individual witch's intent and connection to the natural forces of the earth, it is directed and focused through the proper use of powerful imagery and symbolism. Each witch's power is an expression of their link to the abstract, but the refined art of the witch is to know themselves and others so thoroughly that they become capable of identifying and weaving together all the proper components in order to perform the most potent workings possible.

The steps in executing successful Satanic Witchcraft are simplicity itself however, they require the utmost discipline and direction;

1. You raise the necessary energy.

2. You imprint the energy with your intent.

3. You direct the energy to the desired objective.

4. You release the energy in the desired direction.

There is a scene in episode 11, *Protect the Coven*, of American Horror Story: Coven, which perfectly demonstrates the art of utilizing material components and the fixating of attention in witchcraft. Fiona Goode and Marie LaVeau are working a somewhat complex spell in order to cause havoc and turmoil within a multi-billion dollar corporation which happens to be owned by a lineage of witch hunters who have been aggressively hunting the witches of Fiona's coven. They construct a large maze-like structure meant to be the offices of the enemy company and they place stacks of money and mousetraps throughout the office/maze.

Then, Fiona "baptizes" some white mice in the name of the top individuals working for the business. She sets them free inside the office/maze and utters the proper incantations. As each mouse is caught in a trap, the witchcraft unfolds and the enemy is crushed under the weight of an IRS investigation that halts all corporate activity for them and causes their stocks to plummet. This is an excellent example of the power of our attention and how it can be harnessed, focused and applied to a given end by the intricacies of ritual.

When you begin to direct the power, you should continue to imprint it with your intent while you continually visualize the energy manifesting the end result. To begin with, you must have the energy to work with and the stronger the better. The more concentrated and potent your own energy, the more you will obviously be capable of raising and directing. The more practiced you are, the easier this process becomes. All of this is like working out your physical body. The more you exercise it, the tougher it becomes. You may always employ both your own energy as well as external elemental energies by invoking them as you conduct your work and build up the energy you intend to send forth.

Of course you must also imprint your intention into the energy. By "imprint" I mean you must convey on an abstract level what you want the power to accomplish. Energy all by itself is, for the most part completely neutral and either kinetic or active. During this phase of your working, you must utilize strong visualizations and what I call incantation. Incantations are short and direct expressions that often rhyme and are repeated in order to imprint the energy and keep your focus on the desired end. Present tense must always be utilized since energy does not have the rational power to recognize "will happen in the future" or "did happen in the past." To truly and successfully cause a successful manifestation of your desire, you must envision and feel it as if it is already happening in the here and now.

As a rule, energy always follows the path of least resistance unless it is properly imprinted. For example, many of you want more sex more often. Don't simply insist "more sex is approaching me." This intention could manifest, if not imprinted properly in some awkward sexual situation that simply do not meet the ideal you originally intended or even in something outright unwanted with dire consequences. This happens far more often that one would think. You have to incant and imprint: "frequent and ideal sexual situations will manifest for me now in a very positive and gratifying manner for me." You obviously don't want a faithful friend's wife to suddenly leave them for you or sexual episodes to take place in a way that would be disagreeable in the future.

Some witches prefer to visualize energy as a physical light of some appealing witchy hue. I find that this can initially help if you are having difficulty feeling the power being raised, but keep in mind that a good incantation and visualization of the desired end result will be required along with any other mental device you may choose to use.

So your affirmation would go something like this: "Large amounts of free and easy money are coming to me. This money is all mine to keep and spend as I please. This money is coming to me in a very positive and happy way for me."

Greater, lesser and medial witchcraft are all critical skills that will be combined to varying degrees in the Satanic Witch's forging and stabilization of their personal power. The "balance factor" and fine art of discrimination must be developed and continually employed as we shape the shadows into the dream of our intent.

Lesser Magic is the intentional manipulation of one's behavior and or physical self and environment to achieve a specific effect in one's objective world. Lesser Black Magic is identical to Castaneda's concept of "stalking," as "dreaming" finds its parallel in the ritual chamber of Greater Magic. It is the use of behavior to create shifts in one's own perception as well as in the perception of others. It is also the use of specific behaviors directed at stabilizing and fixating one's point of assemblage after it has shifted to a new position. We have no possibility of successfully creating and sustaining our witchcraft without properly engaging and handling the ordinary consensual world of human affairs.

Dressing, talking and generally presenting one's self in a particular way in order to influence a target audience for a specific end is to use the endless techniques of Lesser Magic. We use this power to gain something for ourselves and we cater its application to that which we seek. Politicians and social climbers are master Lesser Satanic Witches and Warlocks in that they gauge everything about how they appear and how they act in order to elicit a favorable response from others. Politicians are looking for votes and social climbers are looking for power and acceptance. The witch is usually looking for neither of these things unless they have naturally become critical features of their greater quest. For some this may be so. I have so far pursued several different vocations in my life and within each one of these I needed to learn the particular vocabulary of that area of endeavor as well as its rules for achieving success within it. In so doing this I had to learn which manipulative techniques worked best for each unique situation.

The Satanic Witch and Warlock should embody the idea that there is no point in doing a thing unless one intends on doing it well. We are not mediocre beings and do not expend our valuable time and energy involved in thoughts and activities that bear tasteless fruit. Lesser Magic is a mansion filled with powerful tools a discerning warlock may draw from to serve them as they will to whatever ends they pursue.

Required reading for further magnification and study of Lesser Magic and its techniques and applications I recommend The *48 Laws of Power* by Robert Greene and Joost Ellfers. Ultimately, how one chooses to apply Lesser Magic will change according to want, need and the actual objective limitations of one's self and any given scenario. This is where one of the most important black magical maxims necessarily applies. "Know thyself."

The "world" as we have been reared to understand it is composed of a huge catalogue of agreements made between human beings regarding our existence and place within the cosmos. Ordinary human reality in the modern world is largely constructed out of agreements that originate in the social order rather than that of the natural or universal order. We are perpetually three steps removed from experiencing the universe as it is; a forever fluctuating field of energetic awareness. First our primal awareness allows us to perceive a world outside of ourselves, then our physical senses interpret the elements of that world through the limitations of our biological organism, and finally we attribute meaning to the elements or items of the world in terms dictated by their social relevance to us personally and as a species.

Some Terminology

I present here a few terms within the practice of Satanic Witchcraft that I have personally refined in order to create and sustain my own more precise magical lexicon.

Spell:

I use the term spell to refer to an act of magic that requires the harmonizing of some number of separate elements along with the Witch's intent in order to create the ideal condition for a specific desire to manifest. Spells are constructed to focus the Witch's attention in a concentrated manner and then release the build-up of energy towards the attainment of the specified objective. Spells last until the desired objective is achieved and the concentrated energy of the spell rests in the completion of the work. A spell can be a one-time enactment, or it can be a series of actions taken over a specific period of time. Once the objective of a spell has been met, any further magical intervention would have to be re-enacted.

A spell typically requires the use of material components that are used together to create the intended type of resonation required. Spells can be simple or complex according to the needs of the individual Witch.

Hex:

The hex is an act of spontaneous and direct witchcraft. It can be classified as "medial" magic in that there are no material components or long, laborious preparations involved. The hex is the direct channeling of power by the witch for immediate use in whatever capacity and situation they find the need to use it. To hex a person is to call upon the power of witchcraft for certain justice. A good example is the Gypsy hex placed upon Billy Halleck in Stephen King's *Thinner.*

"Medial Magic is a topic and discipline that is rarely if ever explored as a distinct art of its own.

Most will touch and toy with its energies and potentials without knowing what it really is, but very few will grasp its true power and their own ability to wield it as part of their sorcery arsenal. Medial Black Magic is the spontaneous projecting of one's will and intent in conjunction with some form of physical action that is often spontaneous as well. It is of the highest forms of true Witchcraft and its methods and intricacies are always extremely personal. The sorcerer who suddenly utters the inspired words of an incantation into a passing wind to be taken away and made manifest or the Witch who gazes into the flame of a single candle and perfectly projects their will into the rising flame; these are examples of Medial Black Magic in motion. The use of this particular form of sorcery can be found more often among those who we would consider "natural born" wielders of power. While it is true that all human beings do have the capacity for magical achievement, it is equally true that certain individuals are born with and quickly develop a stronger affinity with it. Those who are birthed into this world with an inborn connection with the power of intent often know that they are vastly different from the other human beings around them, and if they reach adulthood successfully they will eventually thrive within their craft.

An act of Medial Black Magic requires only the will of the sorcerer and some means of projecting that will forth. Props are not always necessary; however personal symbols that resonate deeply with the practitioner will act as a magnifier and condenser of power, making the transition from intent to will to form much more direct and efficient. This excerpt from chapter six written by Michael A. Aquino within The Crystal Tablet of Set will further clarify this middle realm between Greater and Lesser Magic.

"However, and this is an important point, Medial Black Magic is not just "making a wish" or "saying a prayer," because these things involve no will, or

even sincerity. Medial Black Magic requires you will that the result you desire actually occurs. Unlike Lesser Magic, there is no calculable cause-and-effect. If you are using proxemic magic (LBM), you can reliably count on keeping someone in a room, driving him out of it, altering his mood, etc. because of the physiological and psychological principles you are applying. As a stage magician (also LBM) you can trick or control people by things that may seem to be Medial Black Magic but aren't. When you resort to Medial Black Magic, you enter that twilight zone between physics and metaphysics. The link may or may not work, or it may work in some unexpected way [not necessarily to your satisfaction]. You may try medial Black Magic and get good, regular results. You may get nowhere and conclude that, for you anyway, it is a waste of time and an intellectual insult. Or you may find it a kind of mix of the two." (Dray, 2013).

Enchantment:

An enchantment is greater witchcraft intended to create a permanent condition of fascination over an individual, place or object. Casting an enchantment requires linking the witch's own power and intent to a greater elemental force that will continue to "power" the enchantment. Historically, an enchantment would entail a pact or agreement between the witch and some type of elemental spirit whereby the witch's intent would be linked to a natural phenomenon such as a waterfall or volcano that was presided over by the elemental entity. The witch would pledge to guard the spirit's abode and in return the spirit would power the enchantment through the kinetic power of the element in question; movement of the waterfall, heat of the volcano, etc. Once an enchantment is sealed it can be used to create a "crossed" or "blessed" condition over a certain location, an aura or power and luck on an object or as is most often the case the appearance of beauty and success over an individual.

Binding:

A binding is a simple yet potent working of witchcraft intended to place a limitation on a target individual. Examples of bindings are poppet spells where the witch ties the hands and feet of their target image together, thus causing them some form of immobility, or workings where a poppet and or personal belongings of an intended victim is placed in water with other ingredients and frozen in a freezer or left to freeze in a small pond before the coming of winter. This type of witchcraft can even be directed at a specific body part as in workings to cause male impotence, or to tie an individual's tongue. Bindings can be as creative as one can imagine but they all basically cast direct and strong limitations on the victim.

Curse:

A Curse is the "calling down" of evil and malediction on an individual or group with the intention they experience long term suffering. The curse is much more than the simple hex and is employed when the witch or warlock wants not only the offender to suffer, but their entire family or immediate personal circle (sometimes for generations). A curse is typically enacted by appealing to wholly demonic forces, but I have also found long term curses can be most effective when appealing to the "restless" dead. For a curse of this nature the witch or warlock will obtain personal items and images of the intended victim and bury them over the grave of a known criminal or even at the site of a horrific battle. The witchcraft here is used to forge a terrible and strong link between the unhappy departed and the living energy of the intended victims. The awareness of the dead can be said to embed itself in the "aura" of the witch's enemy. A curse can also be placed on an item or a physical location and here it works similar to an enchantment.

Bewitchment:

The bewitchment is a form of domination magic and it is used to make slaves out of those it is cast on. To bewitch an individual is to literally take over their mind and senses in order to make them malleable and highly suggestive slaves to the whims of the witch. This is not necessarily an operation used only for lust and sexual gratification, but one employed to gain a helper in every sense of the word. One may bewitch by simple methods such as having the target consume a charmed bit of food or drink, or through more complex methods such as fabricating a hollow wax image of the victim's head in order to fill it with the proper ingredients to cloud the mind, compel action and limit the sight.

These are a few of the more basic operations of Satanic Witchcraft that are most commonly utilized and I certainly intend to expand on more terms and offer a compendium of my own workings in the near future.

-5-

The Focus of Power

I must continue to make one thing extremely clear. The Satanic Witch and Warlock must always remember that all esoteric magical "systems" and mystic paths of "attainment" hold absolutely no intrinsic or objective value and that they were created by human beings. Any of these "traditional" systems of procedural magic are NOT witchcraft, as witchcraft is a spontaneous, creative expression of one's own ability to focus and employ their individual attention and energy in a non-ordinary manner towards the attainment of certain personal objectives.

Unless we claim that a particular divinity has, somewhere in the universe, a concrete corporal actuality in some physical world of their own, then we could possibly understand spirits, gods, demons and devils as beings possessing awareness but having no earthly physicality. "When we are children we are told that the Devil lives in Hell and Hell is under the ground. So, unless we deliberately choose to proceed with knowingly engaging in an erroneous world view, then we either have to acknowledge the existence of inorganic awareness or accept that these various entities do in fact have some type of real, yet incredibly subtle physical existence at a level normally not perceivable by ordinary means." (Dray, 2013).

With this said, every Satanic Witch and Warlock should utilize whatever aesthetic trappings that work best for them to focus their attention for the duration of whatever working they pursue. This can of course change over time however, most of us have our creative foundation crystalized with certain themes and images personal to us and reflective of a particular time in our development. I for instance draw the greatest inspiration from the occult imagery originating during the time period of the early 1960s till about the late 1970s. The images and historical sensory texture of the early Church of Satan years forms the foundation of my primary magical "crystallization inertia." Those of you who are familiar with the literature of Satanism will be familiar with the term ECI. Erotic Crystallization Inertia, which is the life-point at which the individual's erotic nature is permanently formed; a set point that normally will last for the rest of one's life, where the occurrence one's erotic instincts are first stimulated and live in one's memory, vibrant and stimulating as they were at the instant they transpired.

Each of us will have a different set of witchy means and ways to raise our vortex of power. Many will call to the infernal powers, ancient Norse gods or even the fictional pantheons of authors such as H.P Lovecraft or Clive Barker. The crucial thing is to utilize what you actually connect with and what stimulates you the most. I have discovered that work with "the dead" is a constant theme for many Satanic Witches and Warlocks and no matter one's ritual and magical preferences, the legions of the ghostly departed are readily available for sorcerous employment.

Necromancy, as it is traditionally understood is the divinatory art of raising the dead, or the spirits of the dead for the purpose of gathering knowledge considered to be hidden from the living as a natural result of the limitations of material existence. In this conventionally accepted sense, the shades of the departed are believed to exist in a state which grants them the facility for gathering, experiencing and transmitting knowledge in a far superior and boundless manner. In antiquity, necromancers were thought to raise the dead both in spirit, or shadow form as well as bodily as a reanimated corpse. Of course the term necromancy, originating in the ancient Greek language is derived from the Greek work nekros, referring to a corpse and the Greek, manteia meaning a prophecy. At some point during the early middle ages the prefix necro was replaced with the Latin word for black, and the term nigromancy became widely accepted as synonymous with necromancy and both terms subsequently associated with black magic. The identification of necromancy with the more infernal arts of sorcery truly stems from the medieval Christian view that any kind of interference with the body or spirit of the deceased is in extreme violation of god's holy laws and a perversion of the divine natural order. As the religion of Christianity began to dominate the period of late antiquity and the spiritual cosmology of the Catholic Church became widely accepted among every strata of society, the concept of salvation after death made its way into the collective mythologies of the majority of human beings living at that time. As a result of this development a rather rigid view of the hierarchy of the "spirit realm" became established and subsequently the sorcerer, necromancer and Witch were assumed to deal exclusively with lower, inferior non-corporeal entities; for only those spirits who were unworthy of ascension to the higher, heavenly realm would logically be earthbound and available or willing to interact in matters of importance to practitioners of the dark arts.

Of course, by modern standards necromancy would not really fall within the realm of Black Magic or the Left Hand Path in general as they are currently defined. While Satanic Witches and diabolists of every variety can and do employ black magical necromantic operations, this is typically done only in cases where necromantic techniques are simply the most convenient and logical within the overarching framework of the sorcerer's ultimate goal. Necromancy for the Left Hand Path sorcerer is a means to an end which they will use and emphasize according to their own personal predilections, rather than a path embraced in its entirety.

This division of higher and lower spirit life does in fact appear to have become more complex and systematized by the establishment of Christianity and Islam as two of the most dominant world religions, whereas before the advent of these institutions, spirits were generally classified according to locally accepted, traditional pagan beliefs; Good spirits, evil spirits, nature spirits, spirits of the dead, etc. This shift in metaphysical emphasis is important as it developed in complexity and was carried down through history to manifest in almost every form of practice that entails interaction with the human dead.

Any written work involving an in depth study of necromancy and its multitude of applications will necessitate the referencing of an enormous body of information. This can range from the cultural history of cosmological notions concerning the afterlife of human beings, to details on funerary rites or the various branches of spiritism. The objective herein is to emphasize those points of interest within the broad range of the study of death and the sorcery of the dead and to isolate the most common experiential themes as well as practices that are found cross culturally and throughout significant spans of time. Luckily death, dying and the possibility of an afterlife has always obsessed human beings and communicating with the departed has been an aspiration which people have avidly pursued for millennia.

There is certainly no lack of information in this realm and we are fortunate to have the accounts, practices and experience of many talented mediums and magicians to draw from, however the synthesis I seek to achieve will undoubtedly retain the mark of my own personal style shaped by my years immersed within religious and magical systems where I learned the core fundamentals of what would become my own practice in necromantic sorcery.

The major difference with "occult" organizations of the past was that the people who were involved in them were deeply committed practitioners of magic who found these associations vitally integral to their own progress. It really is a shame because there is power in group consensus. I think that the early covens and other groups accomplished a lot during their years of peak group participation. It's possible that there are organizations out there today where good work is going on, but in all honesty I think that most attempts at bringing sorcery practitioners together today fizzle out before they even get any momentum.

If I could choose between a high functioning and solid organization or group or solitary practice, I would go for the group because in black magic cognitive agreements can be formed that lead to a focus of intent, and when this is done in the context of ceremony and ritual much greater power is made accessible. Think of the witch's come of power.

I have had an unusually strong connection to the collective force that most traditions have come to refer to as "the dead" since I can remember, and as with so many other naturally born mediums and necromancers, this connection caused me years of strife in my personal life and particularly as a child and teenager growing up during a time in western society when people popularly regarded the occult or supernatural with a great degree of contempt. Yes, there was a time when taking about the spirit world could instantly turn one into the town pariah or generate vicious, grossly inaccurate rumors about devil worship or Witchcraft.

In the year 1999 I was formally engaged in a process as an experiment in anthropological "immersion" used to develop potential spirit mediumship. Up until this time I had never known that there was in existence any such procedure, but as part of my initial preparation for formal self-initiation as a Warlock, I was lead through a series of planned trials, the key purpose of which was to allow a number of experienced spirit mediums to examine me and to isolate and strengthen both my existing connection to the dead and those spirits that had a close affinity with me.

The tradition that this all took place within is commonly referred to as "espiritismo," "mesa blanca," or white table spiritism. The term spiritism, as opposed to "spiritualism" originated during the late 1800s and is most often attributed to Allan Kardec, who wrote five books that subsequently came to define the spiritist movement. Today, white table spiritism is the direct descendant of the Kardecian spiritist movement, generally employing the use of one or more spirit mediums and a table on which a clean white table cloth is lain along with fresh flowers, clean glasses of water, a crucifix (usually submerged in the largest central water glass), a perfume of some type and any other items the presiding mediums feel need to be on the white altar. Some of the details concerning how the white table tradition developed are lost in time, but the main tenets are still relatively unchanged since the early days of the spirit sitting, or "séance," as it is popularly known.

The Latin American traditions of espiritismo developed alongside of other predominant Afro-Caribbean religious practices and many believe this occurred primarily because of the need to fill the gap left by the absence of the Egungun Cult and priesthood which did not re-establish itself in its original form during the Atlantic slave trade. This specialized society was/is responsible for the propitiation of the ancestors and ensuring their continued remembrance and place within African society. Many traditional African religions were at one time ancestor cults that emphasized the influence of the deceased in the affairs of the living and humanity's proper relationship with the dead. The majority of Africans who were forced into slavery on the Caribbean islands, South America and North America practiced religious traditions that revered the gods, or spirits of nature, as well as the spirits of the dead. This absence of a properly organized spiritual society devoted to taking care of the dead and transmitting its particular ceremonies and rites seems to have created a vacuum of need that was eventually filled through a complex and long process of cross cultural syntheses whereby components of Western European and American spiritist beliefs and practices were adopted and absorbed within the various African based religions.

Because of this fusion of belief and practice, modern espiritismo often contains elements of magical practices typically revolving around healing and cleansing individuals in need of harmful spiritual influences.

The "misa," or mass entails the use of the white table and any number of spirit mediums, some of which might have the ability to demonstrate direct spirit possession. The misas I partook of were centered on my own etheric examination if you will, and the identification and "purification" of those influences from the dead that were most prominent for me. The final "mass" culminated in one last ritual cleansing and a ceremonial "crowning," whereby I was marked as a developed spirit medium so that the shades of the dead could identify me as such and would respond more readily to my beckoning. I will go no further into the history of mediumship, espiritismo, spiritism or the séance as this work is intended to primarily be a book of necromantic sorcery, so while the following material will sometimes depend on a more in depth examination of these other traditions as fundamental building blocks, I shall only touch on them and refer the practitioner to other relevant sources for their own personal study.

Like many others that have gone down this demanding path, I can only relate my experiences in a state of total humility. This is the humility that partly stems from working with and developing an ongoing relationship with the dead and that force we call death. While the Satanic Witch and Warlock should eventually develop a seasoned and sharp confidence in their abilities; abilities gained through decades of both failure and success, they should also have a constant sense of their own innate frailty in the face of those titanic forces they are surrounded by.

Requisite Conditions of the Satanic Witch

There are certain basic conditions the modern witch and warlock must achieve and maintain in order to ensure success in their endeavors. Without the strictest adherence to the behaviors and practical situations that make these conditions possible, it will be very unlikely that one will acquire the necessary experience and energy needed to shift your perception into the twilight realm where successful witchcraft is possible. The conditions that I propose here are the same ones I have established for myself over many years; enough time to repeatedly experience their effects, benefits and implications.

Engaged Solitude

The archetypical image of the witch as a lone entity residing in the most remote regions of the wild is one that finds its root in a prime sorcery truth; this path is a solitary one. Solitude and a solitary existence are more important for the modern witch today than they ever have been in the past however, ours is a specific kind of solitude that arises out of the prevailing conditions we are faced with in the modern world.

Our ancient counterparts who discovered and then organized everything they understood about magic into the foundation we build on today experienced solitude in worldly conditions that were virtually alien from our own. Their perceptual fluidity was superb because the universe they found themselves in was not taken for granted as a fact at the material level. Their cognitive arrangements, personal and social endeavors were not remotely like those of modern people. The ancient witches, and ancient people in general were closer to inner silence as a basic state. The human social inventory was not yet as complex as it would become over time, so consequently the self-dialogue and self-image of these people was infinitely simpler, allowing for an interpretation of reality based less on the individual's sense of identity and more on sensory experience.

Inner silence was a basic condition for ancient witches because they understood and experienced the world around them as a total mystery. Not in any kind of mystical, servile way. They knew they witness something inexplicable, and what they witnessed had not yet been reduced to the complex arrangements of perceptual skimmings that would eventually dominate the cognitive bias of modern people. The ancients lived in natural settings and could withdrawal from ancient society any time they wished. They formed bonds of interest with other witches and together they probed the unknown and found marvels.

We now struggle with certain requirements that came so easily to our predecessors. Inner silence is one of these requirements and solitude is a prerequisite of inner silence. I have carefully chosen the term engaged solitude to capture the experience and state of modern witchcraft practitioners.

The witch exists in a twilight state of artfully synthesized universal contradictions. We seek to transmogrify and transcend our weaknesses, yet we must first know these weaknesses intimately. We seek to embrace the force of life, and yet we must always be aware that the power of our own impending death is so great as to define our very lives and lend incomprehensible power to our acts. I certainly hope you have enjoyed my little introduction to Satanic Witchcraft as much as I have enjoyed writing it. I have a future work in the making at this time and hope those Satanic Witches and Warlocks hungry for some of my own self-constructed spells and rituals will keep an eye out.

The left-handed warlock liberates and re-deploys their existing energy through the use of non-ordinary techniques (witchcraft) in order to experience greater material power and worldly possibilities. This liberated energy is further utilizes in the continued expansion of the self in relation to the material world. We regard the "Nightside" of attention as that vast ocean of perceptual options within our reach, yet inaccessible through ordinary means. On a very basic level, our existing energy is consumed almost in its entirety by our daily concerns. The first step in freeing our energy in the quest for power and expanded awareness is to simply disrupt and free ourselves of these concerns. This is a highly personal task and a generalization cannot be made as to how easy or difficult this will be. First, we have to want this kind of change; a change that initially leads to our personal discomfort on many levels.

Once we have learned to re-focus our attention on things that begin to erode the habit of self-reflection we should immediately and aggressively proceed to the rigorous task of achieving inner silence. Inner silence was a basic condition for witches throughout history because they understood and experienced the world around them as a total mystery. I must emphasize here that the state called inner silence does not entirely entail a cessation of thought. There are levels of silence and factors that can contribute to these states.

We Satanic Witches and Warlocks emphasize and immerse ourselves in the darkness in order to discover its silent secrets. We emphasize the fundamental energetic and material connective nature of our physical bodies and the power that our minds have to shape them according to our will. We emphasize the indisputable fact that our dreams are the gateway to immense personal knowledge, and that by learning to consciously interact while in dreaming, we can begin to acquaint ourselves with our double nature. For the true witch, belief is indeed a means to an end, not an end in itself. This is one of the basic premises of Satanic Magic. The only difference may be in our understanding and application of the power of belief to actually alter the very core nature of what we are. For the black magician, the left hand path leads farther and farther away from what is known to be ordinary humanity. Taking this path costs infinitely more than one might imagine, yet if it is traversed with a mix of confidence and respect it will yield delights undreamed of. In order to begin and sustain the transformation from interested occult student to

Satanic Witch, we have to take real life, concrete and practical measures. Surrounding ourselves with the trappings of magic will not be enough to cause true change in accordance with our well refined will.

The forces the Satanic Witch and Warlock employs are those of their own mind and energy conjoined with that of the earth and elements. The tools we choose to use are either effective channels for our intent or they are simply inadequate props. Our sigils, amulets, potions and herbs amplify energy. This is an energetic statement. Natural material components combined with our own magical link, intensify and transmit energy. This is the entire premise behind the work of a Coven. Covens can be extremely influential in increasing energy, as several extraordinary witches work together to raise and direct these powers in unison. Working alone, the witch or warlock might not be capable of accomplishing certain works. Raising power and directing that energy towards obtaining specific objectives and requirements, is what true witchcraft is all about, not the servile worship of some man-made, imaginary deity.

Runes, glyphs and other symbols are most often equated with witchcraft. There are tools the Satanic Witch will use in order to attract and hold their attention or the attention of others. Astrological timing for raising and guiding energy is frequently central for the success of a working and significantly augments the witch's power. The Satanic Witch and Warlock will use any methods, means and ways they find effective to magnify their powers. This is an important distinction between the Satanic Witch and the traditional Magician or Mystic who is virtually enslaved to the dogma of whatever tradition they uphold and the particular magical texts they blindly follow.

We all know that traditionally witches employ devils in the form of frogs, toads, cats, snakes or other creatures usually referred to as "familiars" to assist them in their evil work, and communicate with them through the intermediate influence of the chosen animal, which was superbly cared for so that a powerful bond could be formed. The familiar gave the witch continual protection and was thought of as a direct gift from Satan. All of nature and all animals are considered highly sacrosanct in Satanism and must always be treated with the greatest respect. Employing Satanic Witchcraft implies working to develop your mind and power

S
A
N
T
A

25085877R00090

Printed in Great Britain
by Amazon